MW00876240

Parenting Chaos

Practical Support and
Encouragement
For Parents of Explosive
Children

Shawna Wingert
Not The Former Things

With many thanks to my sweet boys.
May they always know that they are
deeply loved, just as they are...

You both amaze me.

I first learned the term "explosive child"
in the excellent book by Dr. Ross Greene
– **The Explosive Child.** I cannot
recommend it enough. I am grateful for

his work and his support of parents, just like me.

Parenting Chaos

Practical Support and Encouragement
for Parents of Explosive Children

~ Author's Note ~

The last couple months have brought more meltdowns and explosive behavior in my home than ever before.

My boys are older now.

It looks different. It feels different. It hurts more.

Over and over again, I have been going back to my own blog posts and re-reading **The Explosive Child**, in an effort to remember what I used to know, back when meltdowns happened every day and I was better at them.

In an effort to help myself and maybe, some of you, I have put together this small book with all the information I have ever written (plus a few more tips and tricks that I have never published before).

I wanted something I could grab while hiding in the bathroom or crying in the car. I wanted something that would give me the information and encouragement I needed fast and in the moment.

The truth is, this book is as much for me as it is for anyone else.

With so much love,

Shawna

~ 1 ~

A Little Bit Of Our Story

I am not an expert.

I am not even an experienced parent when it comes to so many of my children's needs.

We received official diagnoses for both of my boys within a year of each other. I think the diagnoses help me to understand them better, although sometimes, it feels like I know even less about how to help them.

The truth is, both of my boys were explosive long before we ever saw a professional or filled out a behavioral evaluation form.

Reality Hurts

I have been scratched, spat on, threatened, punched and called names.

There are holes in the walls, windows that have been broken, iPads that will never be the same and stains on the ceiling that will not come out no matter how hard I scrub.

Our school day often involves more than one book or pencil being thrown, and an anger so fierce I am sometimes afraid.

I am deeply saddened and often ashamed, but it is the truth.

I am parenting explosive children.

Our life is sometimes chaotic and out of control to be sure, but most days are a mix of good and bad, just like anyone else's.

Yes, there are times when I could be more a consistent disciplinarian, but never when one of my sons has completely lost control.

And no, sadly, our family is not all that unusual.

The good news is we are learning slowly, but surely, exactly how to help my sons with <u>explosive behavior</u>.

We are understanding that because of a lack of maturity and function in certain areas, **even the smallest stressors create a fight or flight response as real to him as if he were being chased by a lion.**

And we are finding ways to help them gain control.

If you, like me, are parenting an explosive child, please know, you are not alone.

Just because we don't often publicly discuss the really hard things, doesn't mean they aren't happening.

Parenting Chaos

Throughout this book, I share what's working for us and the realities associated with mothering an explosive child.

I include an in-depth look at how our approach, our day-to-day failures, successes and the progress we are seeing.

I am not an expert, but I live with explosive behavior every single day.

This is a glimpse into our life.

~ 2 ~

Why Is My Child So Explosive?

When my son kicked the windshield, I didn't think it would break.

I was wrong.

Apparently, the force of losing all rational thought and ability was enough to crack it from end to end.

He was crying, flailing and screaming at me.

"I can't do it. Mommmmeeeeeeeee. I can't. I can't go in."

We were in the parking lot of his doctor's office – the very doctor that we needed to see for the increase in his aggressive and violent behaviors.

He had climbed into the front seat as soon as the car stopped and began physically fighting me.

Scratches up and down my arms and on my face, I tried not to cry as feelings of pure defeat and desperation washed over me.

Then he broke the windshield.

We both were stunned.

My son looked at me, suddenly much calmer and said, *"Well, I guess now I have to go in."*

He opened the door, got out of the car and calmly walked into the office.

I have two boys.

A fourteen-year-old and an eleven-year-old.

One loves computers and video games.

The other adores animals and the outdoors.

One is quiet, the other can be boisterous and loud.

My two boys are very, very different from each other.

But there is one thing they have in common.

They are both explosive children.

Over the course of the last ten years, I have been trying to figure out how to react, how to respond, how to discipline, how to show compassion, and how to have boundaries around my children's behavioral challenges.

In the beginning, I listened to all the well-meaning voices.

If you would discipline him more...

He just needs a good spanking....

If you weren't going through a divorce....

He's manipulating you...

*He knows he can get away with it.
That's why he does it.*

I listened and I tried it all.

And none of it, *I repeat*, none of it
worked.

In fact, it got worse.

It's what led us to smashed
windshields in parking lots.

It wasn't until I finally learned more
about my children's neurological
function that it began to make
sense.

Part of it was understanding their
respective diagnoses.

But most of it has been trial and
error, watching and learning,
praying and crying, and more trial
and error.

Please know, I am not an expert in
anything, except my children.

I am not a doctor or a therapist.

I can only share my experience and encourage you that you are not alone.

Experience has taught me that it is impossible to help your child with explosive behavior, without really understanding why he is explosive in the first place.

The truth is, it's hard to start here as a parent. We are told by the culture that we live in (constantly) that our child's behavior is reflective of our ability as parents.

Quite frankly, it feels personal.

And yet, in order to understand the reasons why our children are melting down, it is essential that we set aside any preconceived notion of how this is supposed to be, and instead focus on what is.

Ross W. Greene, Ph.D. says in **The Explosive Child** that parents need to "come to grips" with two important realizations.

The first is:

"Behaviorally-challenging kids need us to take a close look at our beliefs about challenging behavior (beliefs most people don't question unless they're blessed with a behaviorally challenging child) and apply strategies that are often a far cry from ways in which most adults interact with and discipline kids who are not behaviorally challenging." p.5

The second is:

"Behaviorally challenging kids are challenging because they're lacking the skills to not be challenging." p.9

Our children are not explosive to get their way. They are not acting out because they have been spoiled. They are not trying to manipulate us.

There is always, always, always an underlying reason for the explosive behavior, even if we can't yet see it.

Accepting this is the first and necessary step in determining how best to help our children.

Once we do, understanding why our children are explosive becomes much, much easier.

Why Is My Child So Explosive?

I certainly cannot speak for your child. But I can share what I have learned (so far – this is still quite the work in progress around here).

Here are the top contributors to explosive behavior in my family:

Communication Issues

For various reasons, both of my sons struggle with communicating their needs. My oldest has trouble finding words to describe his body and mind. My youngest has unintelligible speech at times, particularly when under stress.

No matter what the reason, communication issues in our home often contribute to explosive behavior.

Sometimes, my boys feel they simply have no other way to communicate their intense, overwhelming needs.

Executive Function Deficits

I know my youngest son is only a minute or so away from melting down when he says he is bored. Boredom for him is not like the usual *"Kids need to be bored in order to be creative. "* When my child says, *"I'm bored,"* what he means is *"I am getting anxious because I don't know what comes next."*

Time and space seem endless to my child because he lacks the executive function to manage his time.

This gap in ability creates stress and often contributes to an explosive reaction.

Another example happened just yesterday with my oldest son. He had a homework assignment to complete with vague directions. He sat in front of the computer for almost an hour trying to figure out where to start. When I came in and asked him how it was going, he completely lost it.

Once he calmed down, I was able to help him figure out the steps to take, but on his own, he was simply unable to get there.

Sensory Input and Overstimulation

This is a big one for both of my children. Because they have sensory processing issues related to noise, smell, light, textures and movement, there are times where their bodies and brains simply become overwhelmed with sensory input.

For example, in a crowded, loud room, my boys both experience a kind of torture that I would not wish on anyone. After a few minutes in this overwhelming environment, a very real "fight or flight" response kicks in and explosive behavior soon follows.

Anxiety

Anxiety is an undercurrent in every single stressor listed above. It also contributes to explosive behavior all on its own for my boys, particularly for my youngest.

When he begins to feel anxious, for any reason (school, bedtime, doctors' appointments, etc.) he very quickly escalates. Because he has an anxiety disorder, he feels an overwhelming threat and fear that I am not sure I will ever completely understand.

As the very real panic sets in, he almost always has a challenging episode.

These are the most common factors that contribute to explosive behavior in my home. Yours may be entirely different, but I do want to make one important point that I think is true for all of us.

As hard as it is to parent an explosive child, I have no doubt that it is significantly more painful to *be* an explosive child.

Understanding why the behavior is occurring is only the first step in helping our kids.

I am a parent, just like you, trying to figure this out.

Let's do it together.

~ 3 ~

Calming My Explosive Child

What's going to happen when he's older and able to do more damage?

Someone is going to get hurt.

What if the neighbors call the police?

I can't do this for the rest of my life.

We don't have the money for another window repair.

At what point do I call 911?

I never thought I could be afraid of my own son.

It is painful for me to admit this, but it's true.

I have had every single one of these thoughts, more than once, over the past few years.

My guess is that if you picked up this book, this list probably feels heartbreakingly familiar.

Having <u>an explosive child is devastating</u> – for me, for my husband, for our entire family.

And the one question we ask ourselves, the doctors, the therapists, and the internet over and over again –

How do I make it stop?

Not just for my sake, but for my suffering child.

Calming An Explosive Child

Please, let me remind you that I am not an expert.

Anything I share is from my own experience, trial and error, tons of prayer, tons of tears, and more trial and error.

I have two boys, both brilliant, funny, and loving.

Both can also be explosive.

For more than ten years I have been struggling to find ways to help my children avoid meltdowns and aggressive behavior.

Here is what I have learned so far.

1. Plan For The Behavior

In our family, the best way to calm explosive behavior has been to plan for it ahead of time.

Here are some examples of what's worked.

Asking How I Can Help

When my youngest son is having a good day, he and I will sit down and draw together.

I ask him what it feels like when he is feeling anxious and overwhelmed. Sometimes, he draws pictures of himself angry. Sometimes, he draws pictures of the things that make him mad. Sometimes, he just stops drawing entirely and talks.

I ask him what he thinks might help when he is starting to feel explosive.

He usually says play with his dog, play in the water, or talk about snakes and take deep breaths. (We've had this conversation enough that it is now a kind of routine.)

When the next explosion occurs, I have his expressed options available to offer as coping skills.

My oldest is a little trickier. He is not as verbal as my youngest and is not really able to communicate how his mind and body feel mid-meltdown.

Instead, he and I talk about what he needs me to do when he is feeling overwhelmed.

Again, he does not respond well to open-ended questions, so my conversation with him usually involves him choosing between two options.

Would you like for me to stay close to you, or do you need to be left alone?

Do you want me to rub your back with deep pressure, or is it better if I don't touch you at all?

Do you want to put on your headphones, or should I just try to keep the house quiet for a bit?

Please note: **For both of my children, there is an assumption that there will be another explosive episode.** My goal in these initial conversations is never to communicate that a meltdown cannot happen again. I have found that telling my children we need to stop this type of behavior just caused more explosive behavior (as soon as they felt it coming on, they panicked, grew more anxious that they would not be able to stop and then exploded). Eventually, when my boys were able to feel some success in calming themselves down (with my help), we saw a decrease in the overall number of meltdowns.

I encourage them in these conversations. This is not about discipline or enforcing rules, it's about coming up with solutions to a very difficult problem. I assure them that I am on their side and that I know we can work together to come up with some things that might help. I tell them I love them, no matter what.

These conversations happen frequently. It's like a check-in to make sure we are on the same page.

Rearranging The Environment

This past summer, every single time my son lost control, he would knock over the chair in our living room. After about the seven-thousandth time picking the dang chair back up and looking at the scratches it left on the wood floor, it finally occurred to me to just move the chair to another room. I also added more pillows and a throw blanket to the couch. I figured if he was going to throw something, at least it would be soft.

The next time my son lost control, there was no longer any furniture to toss. He paced for a bit and then calmed down faster than before.

The same is true for remote controls, electronic devices, and even our TV. After having all of them broken more times than I can count, we now try to keep them out of sight when not in use.

It keeps us from having to replace expensive equipment, and my sons calm down faster if there is less to fuel their explosiveness.

(Incidentally, I saw a cute brass kick-knack the other day on clearance and thought about buying it. I quickly reconsidered when I realized how much damage it could do if one of my sons became dysregulated. You may think this is extreme or even enabling my sons to never learn to control themselves. I respectfully disagree. I did not feel bad about not being able to buy a silly little brass alligator. I felt good about the prospect of all of us having an easier time if one of my sons were to have a meltdown.)

2. Set-Up Predictable Routines

Oh my goodness, this one is easier said than done, but it has been so effective in our home.

Because my children often feel like their bodies and minds are out of control, it makes sense that knowing the day will flow in an expected and controlled manner helps them stay calm.

When our days are chaotic, I can see the decline in my boys' ability to cope.

When our days are predictable, my boys relax a bit and are much more emotionally regulated.

3. Seek Professional Help

Finding the right therapist, doctor or combination of the two can make a real difference in our children's lives.

In our home, it has helped significantly, but not completely.

I've learned that professional treatment is just one aspect of mothering complicated children.

Dealing with explosiveness is no exception.

I used to pin my hopes on the right occupational therapist, or a new prescription. I now know that there is no one thing that cures any of this.

But there are so many things we can do to help.

Seeking treatment is one of them.

No matter what we do, as difficult as it is to parent an explosive child, I imagine it is infinitely more difficult to be an explosive child.

~ 4 ~

My Child Has Lost Control

I heard the sound of glass breaking before I could get to his room.

I ran in, and a book flew past my head and hit the wall behind me.

My son, crying, out of breath, and full of rage, had completely lost control.

He was swinging his arms wildly and pacing.

He was muttering, *"There's nothing to do. There's no way I can fix this. I just want to die."*

The room looked like something on a TV show.

Papers and books, torn and scattered about, were everywhere.

The window was shattered.

For a moment I hesitated. *"It's like stepping into a war zone with landmines,"* I thought.

I took a deep breath and moved towards him.

My son had completely lost control.

Again.

I wish I could say this was an isolated incident. (If you are parenting an explosive child, you know better.)

Unfortunately, both of my boys have struggled and continue to struggle with out-of-control, explosive behavior.

In the moment, it's terrifying.

The mix of anger, fear, and desperation I feel mid-meltdown is not something I would wish on any parent.

The mix of anger, fear, and desperation *my child* feels mid-meltdown is not something I would wish on any child.

In previous posts, I have shared the importance of trying figure out <u>why our children are melting down</u> and how to <u>arrange the environment</u> to help avoid escalating behavior.

Today, I want to share what works for me and for my child, once he has already lost control.

Please know, I am not an expert. I am just a mom, trying to figure out the best way to help my children recover and thrive.

When My Explosive Child Loses Control

De-escalating a meltdown is not an easy task – for me or for my child.

It is physically and emotionally draining.

It's often traumatic.

I am not making these recommendations flippantly, nor with the misconception that this is somehow easy.

It's not.

In fact, helping my children calm down once they are out-of-control is one of the most difficult things I do as a parent.

It's difficult, but it has proven to be worth it.

What To Do, What Not To Do, and How To Help

Here are the steps I take when my child loses control.

Calm Myself First

If I could recommend only one strategy for helping a child that has lost control, this would be it.

The only way I can be effective in helping my son when he is out of control is by showing him that I am in control. This communicates to him that no matter what, it's going to be OK.

In the past, as soon as I sensed my child escalating, I would panic.

As he yelled, I yelled.

When he cried, I began crying.

As he grew increasingly angry, I fumed.

My experience has been, over and over again, that more out of control I feel, the more out of control my son becomes.

Keeping ourselves calm is not an easy step to take, but it is essential.

When it's clear that my son is beginning to lose control, I take a few deep breaths and whisper a quick prayer. (Something like, " Oh God, help me!" Nothing too deep.)

No matter how escalated he becomes...

No matter what is broken....

No matter how I much I want to cry and scream myself...

I purpose to stay calm.

I don't allow myself to think about what happens when he is an adult and could get arrested for this type of behavior.

I don't freak myself out with thoughts like "I can't do this for the rest of my life."

I don't worry about what my husband will say when he gets home and sees the iPad broken (again).

I just focus on my child and what he needs next.

(The honest truth is, in the moment, I pretend like I am a nurse or therapist, and not my son's mom. It's easier for me to approach my son's behavior from a more clinical perspective.)

Once I feel some semblance of being in control of my own emotions, I move in to help my son with his.

Close Proximity and Low Voice

No matter how escalated my son is, I find what works best mid-meltdown is to stay close and use a low, even voice.

I don't touch him or try to restrain him.

I don't speak loudly to be heard over his screams.

I simply stay very close and speak to him in a low, calm, even tone.

If he is starting to inflict pain on himself or me, or is damaging the furniture, walls or windows, I take a defensive pose – again staying close and using a low, calm voice.

In this defensive pose, I pick up either a couch cushion or large stuffed animal. (Incidentally, my son LOVES the biggest, craziest stuffed animals to the point that we aren't sure where to store all of them. The good news is, they are perfect for this type of incident.) I position myself between him and whatever it is that he is trying to harm. If it's the wall, I place the cushion between his foot and the wall. If he is trying to punch or scratch me, I hold the cushion up to defend myself. If he is trying to hurt himself, I place something soft between him and his arm or foot.

Again, any move I make, I do so with a calm demeanor, low voice and in close proximity.

Repeat the Priorities (but nothing else)

I have found that what I say is just as important as how I say it.

What works best is repeating the same few priorities and

encouragement, over and over again.

"I am here with you. I want to help you."

"I will not let you hurt yourself."

"We do not hurt other people."

"We do not damage property."

"You can do this. I know it's hard. I want to help you."

There have been times where I have repeated these statements over and over again, almost melodically, for more than an hour. I find they are much more effective than when I said things like, *"You can't do that!"* *"No!"* and *"You have to stop."*

This took a while for me to get used to. I used to practice what I was going to say ahead of time so that in the moment, I would be prepared.

Assist In The Wind Down With Distraction

No matter how serious the meltdown, there will come a moment when you can physically see and emotionally sense that your child is beginning to calm down.

These are critical moments.

In my experience, one of two things is going to happen next -

My child will either relax and move on, or completely escalate and lose it all over again.

In an attempt to help him do the former, I change my tactics a bit when I see that he is slightly calmer. At this point, I try to distract him.

In the same low voice –

"Let's sit down together and watch that video with the snakes."

"Look at our doggie. Isn't she cute? She loves you so much."

"Do you know that we are having pizza tonight for dinner?"

Bounce Back

Once my child is completely, obviously calm and past the explosive episode, I have found it is essential that we get our day back on track (if I want to avoid any further meltdowns).

This one is tough for me because once my child is calm, I feel exhausted, drained, and ready to go get under the covers for the next ten years or so.

But my child craves consistency. It helps him feel more controlled.

Changing the routine because of a meltdown does not work well for us. Once everyone is calm and settled, I have found it to be imperative that we get back to our normal routine for the day (no Spongebob for four hours so that Mommy can freak out alone in the other room).

The good news is, it helps me feel more in control too.

If you have witnessed this type of behavior, you know it to be true, but I feel the need to stress this anyway –

No one suffers more from explosive behavior than the child himself. No one is more desperate, more confused, or more terrified than a child who has completely lost control of his own ability to function.

Helping our children mid-meltdown is so, so hard.

And it is essential to their overall well-being and growth.

In the moment, these are the ways I have found to help. But decreasing the overall number of explosive episodes requires more than just in the moment care.

I want to encourage you to also consider the other elements we have discussed.

Understanding why our children are melting down and creating a calmer environment for our children are just as important to our overall success.

Your child is not the only one.

There is nothing to be ashamed of.

Shame has no place in loving and caring for our children as they experience some of the toughest moments of their young lives.

It takes time, but it is possible to help our explosive children heal and live well.

My Child Melts Down Every Day, Sometimes All Day Long

My son melted down every single day, sometimes more than once a day, last week.

It was so very sad. And brutal. And destructive. And exhausting. And so very sad.

He has been in a much better place lately, so the *overwhelming, can't control this even when I am trying* feeling of melting down, just made him more anxious and overwhelmed... so he melted down more often and longer.

When he finally calmed down, every single time and through tears, he hung his head and said, *"I am so sorry, Momma."*

My heart felt like it was breaking right in half.

I tried to reassure him – that I know it's not purposeful, that we can replace what was broken, that I just want to help him and am on his side.

I hope he heard me, but through all of his exhaustion and confusion, I am not sure if he did.

I hope he knows I understand more now – although I have to accept that the years of my *not understanding* have paved the way for his apologetic reaction and his feelings of shame.

I hate that I took so long to figure it out.

I hate that I acted in anger and frustration over something that he literally could not control (especially at age 6, at age 7, at age 8…).

I hate that it took me years to even know <u>what a meltdown was</u> – not from my perspective, but from his.

I don't want that for any mom, and I especially don't want that for any child.

Maybe you are like I was, **frustrated and scared, convinced it's your fault and therefore yours to fix**.

It's not and this is for you.

I firmly believe the only way we can really mother our children through meltdowns, is to learn what our children are experiencing first hand.

When my son was first diagnosed, one of the first questions I had for every single professional we encountered – **what do we do when he melts down**?

Not one could really answer.

So, I did Google searches and <u>read books</u> and joined Facebook groups and eventually, met other moms further along in dealing with the same thing. Even better, I eventually met adults on the spectrum who could literally describe it, just like Emma does above.

This information was invaluable.

It changed the way I reacted during a meltdown.

It changed how often he experienced severe meltdowns.

It allowed my son and I to work together, instead of against each other when he experienced a meltdown.

And most importantly, this information, this new learning, allowed me to **better support my son and love him through it all.**

Aggressive and violent meltdowns are awful (*and that might be the biggest understatement I've written*).

They are awful.

They are exhausting.

They are emotionally painful, for my son and for our entire family.

They are so scary, for my son and for our entire family.

They create chaos and destruction that takes days to recover from.

People get hurt. Sometimes physically hurt. Always hurt on the inside.

When my son's meltdowns first escalated, I was beside myself. I was certain it was because I had spoiled him and now he was upping the ante to get what he wanted. Not only that, but everyone else thought that too.

So, we cracked down. We took things away. We grounded. We yelled. We freaked out and melted down right alongside him.

And they just got worse.

They intensified and got more and more out of control.

Before I go any further, I want to share a small but absolutely true list of the damage that was physically done in our home during this timeframe .

I am sharing this list because when we were living with daily meltdowns, I thought we were the only ones.

I thought my son was the only one "this bad".

I would've cried tears of relief if another momma shared the literal mess her life had become at the hands of her child.

So I am sharing mine.

Living With Meltdowns

Numerous holes in walls that needed to be patched and painted again and again.

A handheld video game device thrown with force out of the back window of the car, as we drove down the road and he kicked and screamed. (I am still so grateful that no one on the other side of the street was injured. It simply fell, was flattened by a few cars, and we were out $179.00.)

TV – gone, tipped over and smashed

iPad – destroyed, piece by piece.

Every single thing in his room thrown about in a cyclone of hurt and rage and frustration, landing in a sad broken pile (see picture above)

Every poster, award, and special thing hung on the wall, torn down.

Car windshield smashed, with a broom, in our garage.

Car window smashed, with his feet, as I drove down the road.

His own body, purposefully battered and bruised.

My body, purposely battered and bruised.

His little brother, sometimes bruised, always completely terrified.

Meltdowns are awful.

I hate them.

I hate that they take over his mind and body and we all spin.

I hate that he feels such fear in the middle of them, and such pain once they have passed.

I hate that once one begins, we can try to diffuse it, but sometimes, it just has to run its course.

I hate that no matter how hard they are for me, they are always, always, always worse for my child.

I hate them.

They don't happen as often, not by far. At one point, we had this level of meltdown at least every day, and often two or three times a day. Now, it's only every couple of months.

The progress is a gift. We have all learned to breathe again and relax and find joy in the simple ability to function throughout the day.

And so now, when they come, we are almost surprised (*it's like a strange reminder, "Oh you're still here? I thought you left."*).

Yesterday, my son had a meltdown.

His room was destroyed. He was incapable of logical, functional thought for a good two hours. My heart pounded, his brother grabbed his little dog and hid, and my son cried, "Momm-eeeeeeee, Momm-eeeee, Momm-eeeee," as he rocked back and forth, over and over again. The anguish and lack of control was so clear.

All the same emotions come flooding back, and in the moment, I

felt a familiar helplessness that
breaks my momma heart into
pieces.

And, then it was over.

There is a big difference in how we
now react.

We have learned so much, and
have had years worth of therapies
and meds and books and
websites and speaking with other
families. We are more practiced,
more experienced and more
capable.

And, we know that we likely won't
have another one today, and
tomorrow, and the next day.

We can breathe. We can recover.
We can clean up the mess and
move on.

That's the biggest change. When his
meltdowns first escalated and
became aggressive, we had no
idea if they would ever lessen. In
fact, we lived each day in

anticipation and fear of the next
meltdown.

No longer.

If you are a family dealing with this
every day, I am so sorry. My heart
hurts remembering how suffocating
that feels. It can be so isolating – not
leaving the house, day after day,
because you never know if it's going
to be safe enough to drive
somewhere. Or dropping your child
off at school and then picking them
up with a sense of panic, as you
anticipate what will happen once
you get home.

I wish someone had told me all of
this. I wish someone would've said, "*I
totally understand. My son has
destroyed things too. I've been
physically harmed by one of the little
people I love most in the world. I
would gladly die for him, but it feels
like there is nothing I can do to fix
this.*"

Meltdowns are like a dirty little secret
that moms and dads and even
doctors don't really talk about. **But**

that doesn't mean they don't
happen.

~ 6 ~

Educating My Explosive Child

There were scratches up and down my arms and my mascara was smudged.

I glanced in the rear view mirror and noted that my hair would also need to be fixed before I went into the office.

I looked like I had been in a fight.

The truth is, I had.

As I drove away from my son's school, I fought back tears. *"Just getting him in the door is like a battle,"* I thought. *"How must he feel, having to go to school now for seven hours after starting the day like this?"*

My child was only seven years old.

Two years later, I sat next to him at our kitchen table.

Again there were scratches up and down my arms and his.

Broken pencils littered the floor and his history book was torn in two.

He rocked back and forth, over and over again.

"Just getting him to do a simple history lesson is like a battle," I thought. *"How is he ever going to learn if our lessons are so explosive?"*

We had pulled him from school for a variety of reasons, one of which was this behavior exactly. But bringing him home seemed to increase the explosiveness.

More meltdowns, more stress, more anxiety (at least that I could now see – before, I had the advantage of leaving for the day).

Tears streaming down my son's face and mine, I realized I had to find another way, not just to help him learn but to help our entire family find some semblance of peace.

Public School, Private School, Homeschool – No Matter What, My Child Is Still Explosive

We have been homeschooling both of my boys for eight years now.

After considering all the options (and trying them all) it is what works best for our circumstances.

But it hasn't been easy and it hasn't been perfect.

The first year, I simply recreated a traditional school environment at home. (I even had a bell, that I would ring when it was time to start school and break for lunch.) It was not our best year. Both of my boys hated it.

I hated it.

The second year, we found out what sensory processing disorder was, received an autism diagnosis for my oldest, and confirmed my youngest son's dyslexia and dysgraphia diagnoses. We knew why their behavior could be so out of control but still had no idea what to do about it.

By our third year homeschooling, I was pretty sure I had completely ruined my children.

Every single day was once again a battle, for all of us. Mid-way through, I decided that I would try something totally different for the last half of the year. My thought was that it couldn't really get any worse and if this new approach didn't work, I would put the boys back in school the following year.

They didn't go back to school.

Here's what changed.

What I've Learned About Educating Explosive Children

Life Skills Matter – A Lot!

I spend a large percentage of our "learning time" focused on life skills and coping skills. My assumption is that they need these skills first, and far more than they will need to multiply fractions in the future.

It is encouraging to witness my boys' ability to research topics they are interested in (my oldest son taught himself how to build a computer, part by part, using Google and YouTube). It is a reminder that if I miss something academically, they will know how to get the information they need when they need it.

They cannot, however, learn how to understand their bodies' signals and sensitivities in a YouTube video. They cannot learn social nuances and non-verbal communication in a Google search. This is what I focus on most in their learning.

Movement And Sensory Input Are Important

Regular and frequent breaks, scheduled time in nature, getting outside to walk the dog and get some fresh air – all of these changes to our school routine have helped decrease my sons' likelihood of melting down over learning.

Incorporating sensory activities into our learning (bouncing on the pogo stick while practicing math facts, writing spelling words in soapy water on the ground, taking a ceramics class instead of learning a new language) not only makes it more enjoyable for my boys, it also allows them to retain more of the learning itself.

Rewards Are Not Bribes

I have struggled with this one for years.

I used to feel conflicted about giving rewards for things that my sons should just be doing – like I was bribing my son to do his reading practice. Then his educational therapist reminded me that reading is incredibly challenging for my dyslexic son. She said the way to create consistency was to "over-reward" when he displayed the determination to practice something so difficult.

She was right.

Because our children can often feel completely overwhelmed by even the most basic aspects of life (getting dressed, brushing teeth, dealing with others) rewarding their tenacity in academics is more than reasonable. It makes sense.

The more I reward, the more they participate and learn.

Creating A Learning Lifestyle Is More Effective

Although I started homeschooling believing that I needed to create as close to a school environment at home as possible, I have since completely changed my mind.

Because of the children I have been given, because of the unique needs of our family including frequent doctors appointments and intermittent daily meltdowns, because of my own desire to help my children learn in a way that inspires their curiosity and natural talents, our school day looks nothing like it did in the beginning.

I have found that incorporating learning into our overall lifestyle is what has made the most significant impact in homeschooling my children with behavioral needs.

We have been making this shift for some time, almost by accident. (Meltdowns and chaos will do that to a Type A Momma's school schedule no matter how hard she tries to cling to it.)

This lifestyle of learning allows me to slow down on the days when my children are overwhelmed – and not feel guilty about it. It allows me to not freak out if we go a few days or even weeks without doing math, because we are focused on the basic skills my children need to thrive.

I want our interactions to be about their hearts first, and all the rest can follow. I believe homeschooling is an excellent and viable choice for children who struggle with dysregulation and explosive behavior.

I also believe it is not the only option.

Finding the best possible educational choice for your child is more important than any one ideology or another.

Figuring out a workable educational solution, has made our lives so much more manageable and enjoyable.

I wish the same for yours.

~ 7 ~

The Best Thing You Can Do To Help An Explosive Child

"I am going to write a doctor's note for you stating that you have a serious medical condition. Perhaps this will help you get respite care from someone."

After months of crippling headaches, a stabbing sensation behind my right eye and shooting pains down the right side of my body, I finally went to see a neurologist.

Three MRI's and two blood tests later, she figured out what was wrong with me.

Her diagnosis? I have two children who struggle every single day of their lives.

(Well, and I needed glasses because 42-year-old eyes don't really work as well as 32-year-old eyes. Go figure.)

She literally wrote me a doctor's note for rest.

I left the doctor's office that day with one pressing thought- **not taking care of me was taking its toll on all of us.**

I had known it to be true for some time.

I heard myself snapping at the boys when they grew dysregulated. I felt myself crumble and cry when my youngest threw something at the wall.

The more explosive the behavior, the less equipped I was the deal with it – exactly the opposite of what I knew we all needed.

It's easy to get caught up in it all. Daily meltdowns, hourly meltdowns, all night long meltdowns are destructive in more ways than the damage our children do to the walls or the car windows.

In my case, the meltdowns had taken over our entire lives, including my own ability to care for myself. The doctor's note was a wake-up call.

My children needed me to be at my best, not my absolute, bottom of the barrel, barely scraping by worst.

Moreover, when did I stop thinking of myself as a person? A person needing basic levels of rest, care and love?

The Best Thing You Can Do To Help An Explosive Child

Part of figuring out this life is figuring out how to tackle what might be the most difficult and most important thing we can to do help our explosive children.

To really help our children, we have to care for the person they rely on most.

Self-care, when you have children who struggle with explosive behavior is not a luxury. It's a part of the treatment plan.

Here is what I am learning about taking care of myself so that I can better take care of my children and their needs.

Accept That It Is Not All In Our Control

This is, by far, the most important thing I can share about how to really care for ourselves in all of this. It's not a massage to schedule, or a friend to call, or a sleep routine to implement. It's far more important than that.

In order to really be able to take care of ourselves, it is critical that we acknowledge that we cannot control

everything that happens with our kids.

Sometimes, they are going to meltdown.

Sometimes, they will not be able to engage the way we need them to.

Sometimes, they will be explosive and dysregulated, despite our best efforts to help.

Part of the danger in sharing a series like this is believing that I somehow (or you somehow) can make all the tough days go away. Yes, there are so many things that can help. But sometimes, our children's experience will be what it is going to be no matter what we do.

And accepting this is OK. In order to allow ourselves the self-care we desperately need, we have to start here.

It is not our job to fix anything.

It is our job to help when we can and love fiercely when we can't.

I am learning that an element of loving fiercely is making sure the person that cares for them is healthy and capable.

Just Do The One Thing

Part of me taking care of myself has been prioritizing one thing that I know makes the biggest difference in my overall well-being.

For me, this is getting time away with my friends every once in a while. A dinner out, a trip to the spa, a night away at a hotel watching movies and sleeping more than usual – **all of these are really difficult to work out in my life.**

But they are what ground me, remind me who I am and give me the time and space to breathe and feel like a person again (and not just a caregiver). I have had to get creative to manage the time and

money to do this every few months,
but it has been worth it for my entire
family.

My husband gets his wife back
refreshed.

My sons have a more patient and
loving momma.

And I feel like God has showered me
with grace and love through the
wonderful women He has placed in
my life.

Sleep

Sleep is really, really hard to come
by around here. It has been for 15
years and I still don't really have
great advice.

But the truth is we have to sleep. It is
a biological fact.

Sleep deprivation is used as a form
of torture in war-torn areas. I
understand why.

Without sleep, everything is more difficult. Without sleep, I am less likely to be able to stay calm and do all the things I need to do to help my children cope.

Sleep is a huge element of self-care, but the one that is the most elusive for me.

The only thing I have found that works in seasons where my children are struggling at night and need me, is sacrificing everything else in order to get naps during the day.

This means the dishes will pile up and I will allow my boys to play video games for as long as they can sit still (which, incidentally, is never really as long as I hope) while I nap for 20 minutes or as long as they will let me.

This means that on the weekends, my husband will necessarily take over and I will sleep.

I find that sacrificing everything else for my own rest helps me and my children more than any other aspect of self-care.

Enjoy Your Other Children

Sometimes, when one of my boys is having a particularly difficult time, part of self-care is getting time alone with the one who is not struggling.

There is something very special about taking an hour and going to ice cream to reconnect with a child who is being left out in the midst of explosive meltdowns and aggression.

It's good for my son and it's good for my momma's heart to just do something sweet and "normal."

I absolutely consider this an element of my own self-care.

Leave Anyway

There will be times that your child is clinging to you as you walk out the door.

There will be times that your child is melting down and raging as you grab your keys.

There will be times that you cry in your car all the way to the spa because your son was so dysregulated but you left him anyway, knowing that you could help and your husband probably won't be as capable.

My advice?

No matter how much guilt you feel, no matter how much the hypervigilance is making your heart pound, no matter how much you are worried about your child's explosive behavior in your absence –

Leave Anyway.

We have to, have to, have to take care of ourselves. We are human beings. We are not caregivers or therapists that go home at the end of the day. There is no finish line in this life we lead. We have to find short breaks along the way.

Please allow me to say this again –

Self-care, when you have children who struggle with explosive behavior is not a luxury. It's a part of the treatment plan.

All the other recommendations and tips for parenting explosive children in this series will not matter if you are not equipped to do them.

You are a person, independent of your child.

You are more than the meltdowns, the mothering, the cleaning up, the doctors' appointments, and the therapies.

You matter.

Please take good care.

~ About The Author ~

Shawna Wingert writes about motherhood, special needs and the beauty of everyday messes at www.nottheformerthings.com.

She is a special needs advocate, speaker, and writer

and has participated in parenting discussions on Today. com, Simple Homeschool, Autism Speaks, The Mighty, For Every Mom, and The Huffington Post. She is the author of two books, Everyday Autism and Special Education at Home.

Shawna lives in Southern California with her voice actor husband and two awesome sons.

Made in the USA
San Bernardino, CA
07 March 2019